D0604872

MAJOR LEAGUE BASEBALL® HOMETOWN HEROES™

The Most Outstanding Players in Baseball History, Club by Club

★

FOREWORD BY TIM KURKJIAN

MAJOR LEAGUE BASEBALL PROPERTIES, INC.

BALLANTINE BOOKS • NEW YORK

Published in the United States by Ballantine Books,
an imprint of The Random House Publishing Group,
a division of Random House, Inc., New York.

Developed, written and designed by MLB Publishing,
the publishing department of Major League Baseball.

BALLANTINE and colophon are registered trademarks
of Random House, Inc.

ISBN-10 0-345-49833-X
ISBN-13 978-0-345-49833-5

Printed in the United States of America

www.ballantinebooks.com

9 8 7 6 5 4 3 2 1

First Edition

ACKNOWLEDGMENTS

MORE THAN JUST EMPLOYEES, EVERYONE IN THE PUBLISHING AND PHOTOS DEPARTMENT OF Major League Baseball is a huge fan of the game. So, cliché or not, this book really was a labor of love, the fruit of numerous individuals working tirelessly to put together a historic record of Hometown Heroes.

There are so many people who should be recognized for their role in creating this book. We would like to thank the Major League Baseball Corporate Sales and Marketing Group and DHL for joining forces to create the Major League Baseball Hometown Heroes campaign, the inspiration for this product. And without the help from Jennifer Osborne, William Takes, Mark Maguire and the rest of the talented team at Random House, our partners on this publishing venture, this book simply would not have been possible. And David Jones, who has long been one of our favorite baseball historians to work with, supplied a talent and detail to the writing and researching of this book that really brought all of the Hometown Heroes—whether Rusty Greer or Babe Ruth—to life.

Lastly, this book contains so many players and so many achievements. It's a credit to them that the skilled hands of the staff of Major League Baseball Publishing and Photos, truly the best in the business, were able to honor their careers with a product that suits them. —THE EDITORS of MAJOR LEAGUE BASEBALL

Major League Baseball Publishing: Vice President, Publishing: Donald S. Hintze; Editorial Director: Mike McCormick; Publications Art Director: Faith M. Rittenberg; Senior Production Manager: Claire Walsh; Associate Art Director: Christina McCormick; Associate Editor: Jon Schwartz; Project Designer: Gail Ghezzi; Project Editorial Assistants: Anamika Chakrabarty, Nathan Maciborski, Dan Rosen. **Major League Baseball Photos:** Director: Rich Pilling; Photo Editor: Paul Cunningham.

PHOTOGRAPHY

JACKET: Clockwise from top left: NBLA/MLB Photos; Rich Pilling/MLB Photos; Louis Requena/MLB Photos; NBLA/MLB Photos; Photo File/MLB Photos; Michael Zagaris/MLB Photos; Mitchell Layton/MLB Photos; Louis Requena/MLB Photos; Rich Pilling/MLB Photos; Louis Requena/MLB Photos. INTERIOR: Rich Pilling/MLB Photos: 21, 22B, 25, 26T, 42T, 43T, 49, 52, 53, 86T, 90T, 91T, 91B, 93, 97, 98T, 98B, 105, 106B, 117T, 121, 122, 125, 127, 135, 137B, 144B; Louis Requena/MLB Photos: 10BR, 27T, 27B, 29, 31B, 37, 38B, 46, 47, 54, 67, 73, 89, 90B, 95T, 99T, 99B, 103B, 109, 126, 128, 136T, 144T, 145T, 155; NBLA/MLB Photos: 30B, 39B, 75, 78T, 78B, 79T, 79B, 107T, 113, 123, 139, 140B, 148T, 149T, 151, 154; Photo File/MLB Photos: 45, 55, 66, 69, 77, 106T, 107B, 110, 129, 141T, 145B, 149B, 152; MLB Photos: 35T, 48, 68, 74, 136B, 140T, 153; Michael Zagaris/MLB Photos: 31T, 58B, 62T, 82T, 87T; Brad Mangin/MLB Photos: 63T, 72, 82B, 83T, 83B; John Williamson/MLB Photos: 116T, 116B, 117B, 131, 137T; Ron Vesely/MLB Photos: 33, 115, 143, 148B; Bettmann/Corbis: 10L, 11T, 17, 159; Diamond Images/Getty Images: 42B, 51, 103T; Mitchell Layton/MLB Photos: 94T, 94B, 95B; Robert Beck/MLB Photos: 30T, 102B; Mike Fiala/AFP/Getty Images: 61, 63B; Tony Tomsic/MLB Photos: 71, 112; David Greene/MLB Photos: 81, 87B; Heather Hall/AFP/Getty Images: 9; Focus on Sport/Getty Images: 10TR; Ezra Shaw/Getty Images: 11B; Rick Stewart/Getty Images: 12-13; Underwood & Underwood/Corbis: 14; Bernstein Associates/Getty Images: 22T; Otto Greule Jr./Allsport: 23T; Donald Miralle/Getty Images: 23B; Ronald Martinez/Getty Images: 26B; Craig Melvin/MLB Photos: 34T; Joe Williams/MLB Photos: 34B; Rob Skeoch/MLB Photos: 35B; Jamie Squire/Getty Images: 38T; Scott Cunningham/Getty Images: 39T; Allsport/Getty Images: 41; Jonathan Daniel/Getty Images: 43B; Robert Rogers/MLB Photos: 57; Nick Laham/Getty Images: 58T; Jeff Gross/Getty Images: 59T; David Seelig/Allsport: 59B; Jeff Haynes/AFP/Getty Images: 62B; Nat Fein/MLB Photos: 65; Eliot J. Schechter/MLB Photos: 85; John Grieshop/MLB Photos: 86B; Jon Soohoo/MLB Photos: 101; Rob Leiter/MLB Photos: 102T; Klinger Smith/MLB Photos: 111; The Brearley Collection/MLB Photos: 119; Bill Polo/MLB Photos: 120; David Blank/MLB Photos: 132T; Karl Gehring/MLB Photos: 132B; Eric Lars Baake/MLB Photos: 133T; Bill Sallaz/MLB Photos: 133B; John Reid III/MLB Photos: 141B; Stephen Green/MLB Photos: 147; Morris Berman/MLB Photos: 156; Earl Richardson/Allsport: 158; Christopher Ruppel/Allsport: 160.

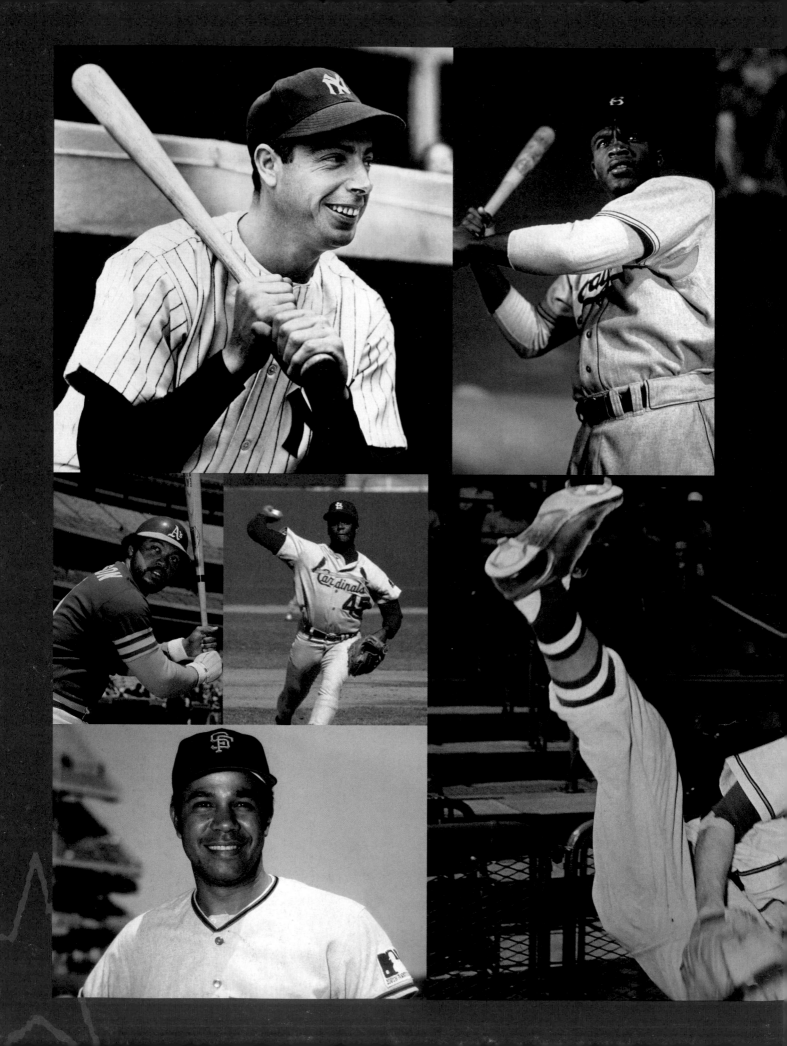

CONTENTS

FOREWORD

BY TIM KURKJIAN

THE 22-MINUTE STOPPAGE OF PLAY ON SEPTEMBER 6, 1995, AT ORIOLE PARK DEFINED

a Hometown Hero. Baltimore shortstop Cal Ripken Jr., who became baseball's Iron Man that

night, took an unforgettable lap around the ballpark. He shook hands with fans, many of whom

were weeping, he pointed at others because he knew them, or knew their face. He patted his

heart several times, overwhelmed by the outpouring of love. He hugged his wife and children

as if he hadn't seen them in years. It was a night about more than just baseball; it was about

all that was right with the game. It was about family, neighborhood, commitment and grace.

That's a Hometown Hero. There have been many of them in baseball—more than you might

think. Third baseman Brooks Robinson, another Baltimore icon, is a Hometown Hero because

of his remarkably charitable ways with people, including with the average guy who just

wants to shake his hand. In the late 1970s, Gordon Beard, a sportswriter from Baltimore, made a speech at an Orioles banquet. "In New York," he said, "they named a candy bar after Reggie Jackson. Here in Baltimore, we name our children after Brooks Robinson."

Stan Musial is a Hometown Hero in St. Louis not because of his .331 career average, but because he plays "Take Me Out to the Ballgame" on his harmonica at events big and small. Ozzie Smith earned the title because he did a backflip every year at Busch Stadium as he ran onto the field for the home opener. Willie Stargell's "We Are Family" slogan for the 1979 world champion Pirates, and Bill Mazeroski's rounding third with his hat wind-milling in 1960 have made them Hometown Heroes.

A Hometown Hero is Roberto Clemente's relief effort for Nicaragua on that fateful New Year's Eve in 1972. It is Albert Pujols, who is always looking to help kids in the community.

Jackie Robinson was such a big Hometown Hero in Brooklyn that when he was traded across town to the hated Giants, he retired rather than report. He was accepted by the Dodgers thanks to the support he got from another Hometown Hero, shortstop Pee Wee Reese.

A Hometown Hero has the dignity Hank Aaron had as he carried himself during his difficult chase of Babe Ruth, and the smiles of Ernie Banks

Brooklyn fans loved Jackie's (left) hustle.

Clemente's (top right) character endeared him to Pirates fans.

Cards fans adored the quirky Musial (bottom right).

Brooks (opposite, top) flashed some leather with the O's.

And Piazza (opposite, bottom) will always be welcomed at Shea Stadium.

and Kirby Puckett. Jeff Bagwell and Craig Biggio, who played on the right side of the infield every time, are Hometown Heroes. It's Warren Spahn, who was on the Bridge at Remagen when United States troops entered Germany for the first time in World War II. It's Jim Abbott, a one-handed pitcher who wanted no one to pity his disability, which no one did that day in Spring Training when he pitched well—and hit a triple.

A Hometown Hero is former Mets catcher Mike Piazza, who received a standing ovation when he returned to Shea Stadium for the first time as a member of the Padres in 2006. After he homered off Pedro Martinez, Piazza got a curtain call. It's Ted Williams helping to start the Jimmy Fund in Boston. It's Jay Buhner and his "Buzz-Cut Night" in Seattle; thousands got their heads shaved to look like the Mariners right fielder. It's the rally fans held in downtown Denver to convince Rockies management to keep outfielder Dante Bichette.

A Hometown Hero is Lou Gehrig, whose record 2,130 consecutive games played streak was broken by Ripken. Gehrig's famous farewell speech at Yankee Stadium—*"Today I consider myself the luckiest man on the face of the earth"*—is why Ripken's lap around the park had such meaning. "Luckiest"? *We* are the lucky ones, for having the chance to share a small part of the careers of Gehrig, Ripken and every other Hometown Hero who has had a chance to leave his mark on the game. ★

Ripken is still an icon in Baltimore because of the way he always made time for the fans.

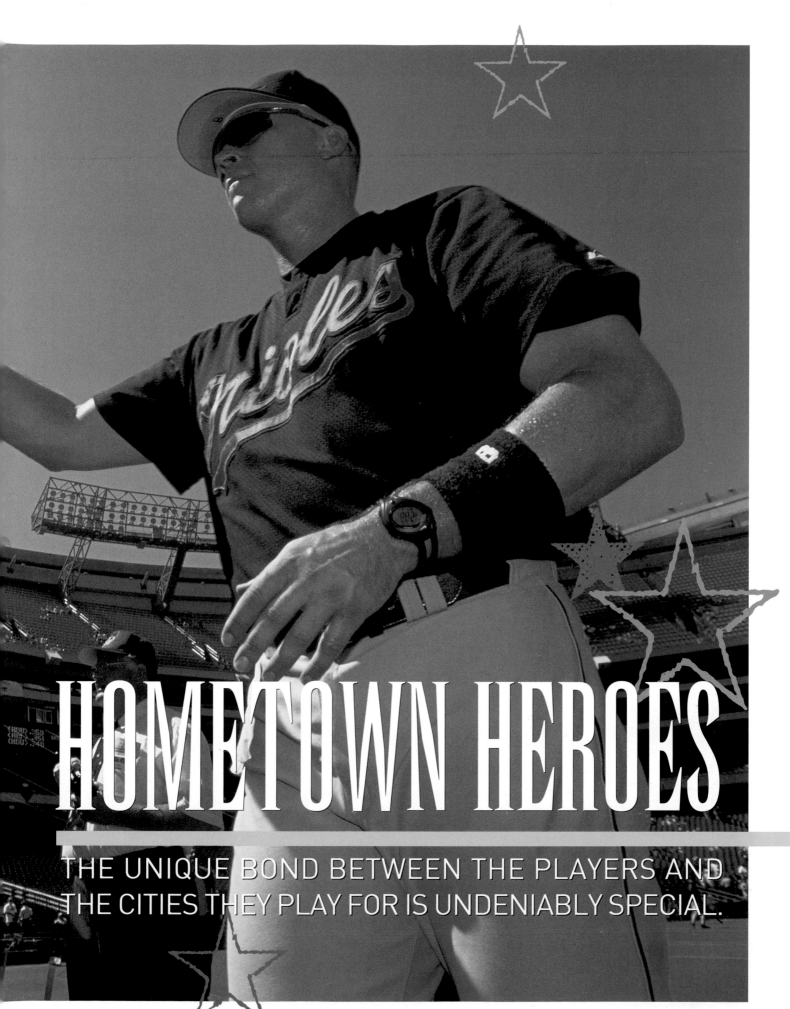

HOMETOWN HEROES

THE UNIQUE BOND BETWEEN THE PLAYERS AND THE CITIES THEY PLAY FOR IS UNDENIABLY SPECIAL.

13

From bonding with fans in Idaho to his days in Washington, Walter Johnson was always a fan favorite.

THE WEISER, IDAHO, TRAIN DEPOT WAS MORE CROWDED than usual on July 22, 1907, as the town's baseball fans came out to wish their 19-year-old star pitcher farewell. Although the youngster was born in Kansas, raised in California, and spent just a bit longer than one season in the small mining enclave near the Oregon border, he already had become a local legend, a hero to the community's fans, who warmly called him "Pardner" when they passed him on the street. As the train prepared to take the pitcher to his Big League destination, the townspeople begged him to stay, even offering him a cigar store. But Walter Johnson, who would go on to rewrite the record books in his 21 years with the Washington Senators, tearfully refused. "You know how you are at 19," he later explained. "You want to see things."

season, even if that relationship lasts only a few months. After all, it took just one swing of Joe Carter's bat in the 1993 World Series for the slugger to become a hero in Toronto, and Curt Schilling's bloody sock during the 2004 postseason cemented his legacy in Boston.

How much more special, then, are the relationships that develop and mature over the course of many seasons, sometimes encompassing a player's entire career? Such ties bind tighter than does the fleeting satisfaction of a world title or a Most Valuable Player Award. "You don't get a ring for it. You don't get a trophy for it," Banks says of his relationship with the city of Chicago, borne out of the 19 seasons he spent patrolling the infield at Wrigley Field. "When I started playing, the grandparents of the

> Being a **Hometown Hero** means more than fans knowing your stats. It means knowing the way a **player** stands at the plate, the way he **fidgets** with his batting gloves, the way he runs the **bases.**

Forty-four years later, a young shortstop named Ernie Banks experienced a similar send-off across the Atlantic, from the German port town of Bremerhaven. It was 1951, three years before Banks's rookie season with the Cubs, but the locals took to the skinny 20-year-old from Texas, who starred for an Army team stationed in the war-torn country. "I was a Hometown Hero," Banks says of the year he spent in Germany. "They wrote a lot of stuff about me in the paper." More than 50 years later, Banks still can recall the contingent of fans who saw his ship off at Bremerhaven: "They were singing that song, 'Auf Wiedersehen, Auf Wiedersehen.'"

Johnson's love affair with the town of Weiser and Banks's fond recollections of his experiences in Germany demonstrate the special bond that can develop between a player and the place he calls home during a baseball

children that are coming to Wrigley Field now were coming to Wrigley Field then. It's family. It's really family. That's what my relationship is with the city of Chicago."

"FAMILY." IT'S THE ONE WORD THAT CAN CAPTURE THE unique bond between a player and a town that creates a Hometown Hero. It's more than stats. Plenty of great players have had gaudy averages in a city, only to split when their contracts expired. Becoming a city's favorite son requires traits that resonate with a town's cultural identity.

During the 1930s, Joe DiMaggio became a hero to New York's vibrant Italian-American community. Twenty years later, Al Kaline's lunch-pail approach to the game melded perfectly with Detroit's blue-collar lifestyle. During the mid-1970s, a young Robin Yount discovered that Milwaukee's small-market charm provided the perfect home.

"I was a pretty shy kid at that stage and certainly didn't need the attention," Yount recalls. "We were pretty much under the radar in Milwaukee for a long time, and that kind of fit my personality just fine." Yount's career blossomed in Milwaukee, even though championships eluded the Brewers during his 20 seasons in the Cream City. Yount admits that he considered leaving near the end of his career to pursue his dream of competing for a title, but loyalty to the organization that had sheltered him for the better part of two decades eventually overrode all other factors. "When I put everything on the scale, it weighed a lot heavier on the Milwaukee side."

Postseason experience famously eluded Banks throughout his career in Chicago, but today the Hall of Famer adopts a different philosophy. "Winning is unlimited," he says,

Stadium during the 1942 season, the Fenway Park faithful sometimes jeered at Ted Williams, and Mike Schmidt had his run-ins with Philadelphia fans.

Yount can recall being booed in Milwaukee when he was mired in a slump at the plate or the team wasn't doing well, but he says he never took it personally. "Sometimes a player deserves it, because he isn't playing his best and that's what the fans want to see," Yount says. "You always knew that the fans were behind you in Milwaukee. Even if you were in rough times, [the booing] never felt like it was vindictive in any way."

SUCH IS THE TRUST THAT CAN BE BUILT OVER THE course of a player's career when he stays with one team, in one city—a phenomenon which many believe is

It took just one **swing** of Joe Carter's bat in the 1993 World Series for the **slugger** to become a **hero** in Toronto, and Curt Schilling's bloody sock during the 2004 **postseason** cemented his Boston **legacy.**

reflecting on the Cubs fan who was a doctor and spotted Banks in a Chicago hospital, noticed that his arm was swelling from an infection, and rushed Banks into surgery, probably saving his life. "This was a guy who came to Wrigley Field and saw me play. That's winning."

As Banks discovered, being a Hometown Hero means more than having fans who know your stats. It means fans who know the way a player stands at the plate, the way he fidgets with his batting gloves between pitches, the way he runs the bases. These fans also know a player's weaknesses: his tendency to pop up pitches thrown in on his hands, his difficulty at reaching ground balls hit to his left side, or his habit of grounding into double plays. When a relationship between a player and a city lasts long enough, it's bound to have its own squabbles and passing feuds. DiMaggio was booed at Yankee

in decline. As George Brett, who spent all 21 years of his Major League career with the Royals, once noted: "It means something to me, and hopefully the fans, to flip my [baseball] card over and see only one team and one city. That doesn't happen a lot anymore, but it should."

Many point to Cal Ripken Jr. and Tony Gwynn, who spent their entire careers in Baltimore and San Diego, respectively, as the last of a dying breed: the player whose loyalty to his team and city outweighs the lure of free-agent lucre. "You're still going to have Hometown Heroes," Yount says. "Just look at Derek Jeter in New York. But [with free agency] I don't think the city gets to know the individuals, or develop the same love affair with the team, because the faces are so different year in and year out. In a way, I don't think that's in the best interest of the game."

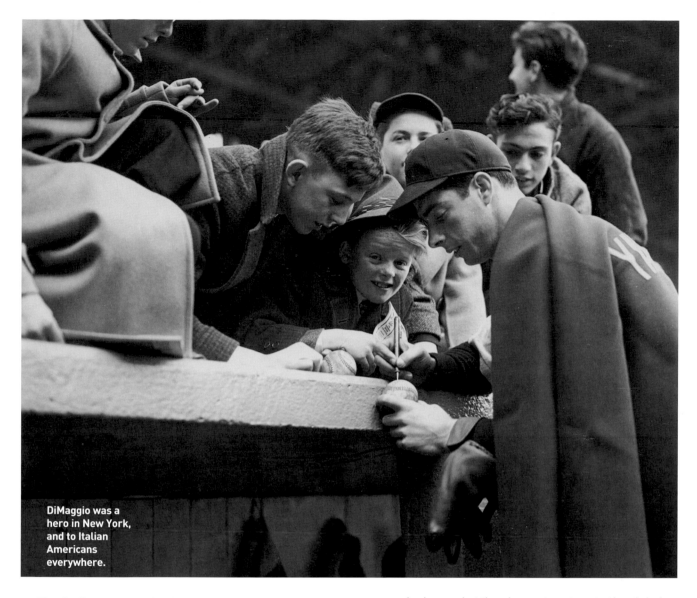

DiMaggio was a hero in New York, and to Italian Americans everywhere.

The decline in player loyalty may be as much about perception as reality. While free agency has given players the freedom to pursue a change of scenery, there has been a simultaneous decline in the number of trades. The result is that players today actually stay in the same place about as much as previous generations. After the 2006 season, for example, there were 22 players who had been with the same club for at least 10 years. In 1966, there were 20 such players. Granted, there are now 10 more teams in the Bigs than 40 years ago, but the numbers show that player loyalty hasn't declined as much as some had feared.

Even when players do play for multiple teams, the ties that bind them to their original clubs often bring them back. Harold Baines spent his first nine and a half seasons in the Bigs with the White Sox before being dealt in 1989. When he became a free agent following the 1995 season, he jumped at the chance to return to the club that gave him his start. "I always felt that I never left," Baines says. "When I came back it was overwhelming for me that [the fans] still remembered me as being part of the team."

Regardless of player movement, the love for the game that unites fans and players means that Hometown Heroes will continue to pop up wherever baseball is played. During his Hall of Fame career, which spanned 25 years, Texas-born Negro Leagues shortstop Willie Wells played in places as disparate as Detroit, St. Louis, Newark, Baltimore and Cuba, but found true happiness in Veracruz, Mexico, where the local fans knew him as *"El Diablo."* "We are heroes here, and not just ballplayers," Wells wrote at the time, reflecting the enduring appeal of a sport that still has the power to break down every kind of barrier. For proof, just go to a ballpark near you. ★

THE NOMINEES

★ ★ ★

MAJOR LEAGUE BASEBALL®
HOMETOWN HEROES™

ANGELS

★ ★ ★

ENGLISH PUNDIT G.K. CHESTERTON ONCE QUIPPED THAT

"The reason angels can fly is because they take themselves lightly."

Fitting words for a franchise that grew up as the pride and joy of

a Singin' Cowboy and achieved its first world championship with

the aid of a Rally Monkey. Over the past 45 years, Angels fans have

been dazzled by the overpowering heat of Nolan Ryan and the

spectacular catches of Jim Edmonds, but they have reserved a spe-

cial place in their hearts for mainstays like Chuck Finley and Tim

Salmon—men who carried the franchise through some of its biggest

disappointments and also saw it through to its greatest triumphs.

ROD CAREW

★ Collected 3,000th career hit on August 4, 1985

★ Batted franchise-best .314 in seven years with Angels

★ Voted All-Star Game starter every year from 1979 to 1984

★ Batted .412 in 1979 ALCS

★ Hit in then–club record 25 straight games in 1982

JIM ABBOTT

★ In 1989, went directly from college to the Major Leagues

★ Pitched Team USA to Gold Medal at 1988 Olympics

★ Tossed a no-hitter on September 4, 1993

★ Led Angels with 2.89 ERA in 1991

★ Once hit a ball 400 feet during 1991 Spring Training game

DON BAYLOR

★ 1979 AL MVP

★ Drove in team-record 139 runs in 1979

★ Established record with 10 RBI in 1982 ALCS

★ Hit by 267 pitches in his career, fourth most all-time

★ Became first free agent to sign with Angels in 1976

CHUCK FINLEY

★ Won club-record 165 games in Angels uniform

★ Led team in ERA nine times

★ Placed among league leaders in strikeouts 10 times

★ Led AL in innings pitched in 1994

★ Struck out four batters in an inning twice in 1999

TIM SALMON

★ Holds Angels career home run and runs scored marks

★ 1993 AL Rookie of the Year

★ Homered twice in Game 2 of 2002 World Series

★ Named 2002 AL Comeback Player of the Year

★ Selected Angels Team MVP three times

ASTROS

★ ★ ★

FROM THE RAINBOW-COLORED SEATS OF THEIR FIRST BALLPARK

to the kaleidoscopic uniforms of the 1980s and the challenging

topography of Tal's Hill, the Astros have embraced diversity through-

out their history. Appropriately, Houston's best players also have

run the spectrum, from fireballing hurlers J.R. Richard and Nolan

Ryan to fearsome sluggers Glenn Davis and Lance Berkman. But

undoubtedly the two players most often associated with the franchise's

history are Craig Biggio and Jeff Bagwell, two potential Hall of Famers

who have spent the last 16 seasons as teammates, helping the Astros

win four division titles and the 2005 National League pennant.

NOLAN RYAN

★ Threw fifth career no-hitter on September 26, 1981
★ Won NL ERA titles in 1981 and 1987
★ Led NL in strikeouts in 1987 and 1988
★ Broke Walter Johnson's career strikeout record on April 27, 1983
★ Holds club record with 1,866 career strikeouts

JEFF BAGWELL

- ★ 1994 NL MVP
- ★ 1991 NL Rookie of the Year
- ★ Holds club record for career and single-season home runs
- ★ Posted a club-record .368 batting average in 1994
- ★ Scored 152 runs in 2000, more than any player since 1936

CRAIG BIGGIO

- ★ Astros hits record holder for career and single season
- ★ Seven-time NL All-Star
- ★ Four-time Gold Glove Award winner
- ★ Holds club record for runs scored
- ★ Ranks second all time in career hit-by-pitches

LARRY DIERKER

★ In 1969, became club's first 20-game winner

★ Threw no-hitter on July 9, 1976

★ Made Major League debut on 18th birthday

★ Holds club record for career shutouts

★ 1998 NL Manager of the Year

JIMMY WYNN

★ Led Astros in home runs every year from 1965 to 1970

★ Nicknamed "The Toy Cannon"

★ Became first Astro to hit three homers in a game on June 15, 1967

★ Led NL outfielders in putouts in 1965 and 1967

★ Uniform No. 24 retired in 2005

ATHLETICS

★ ★ ★

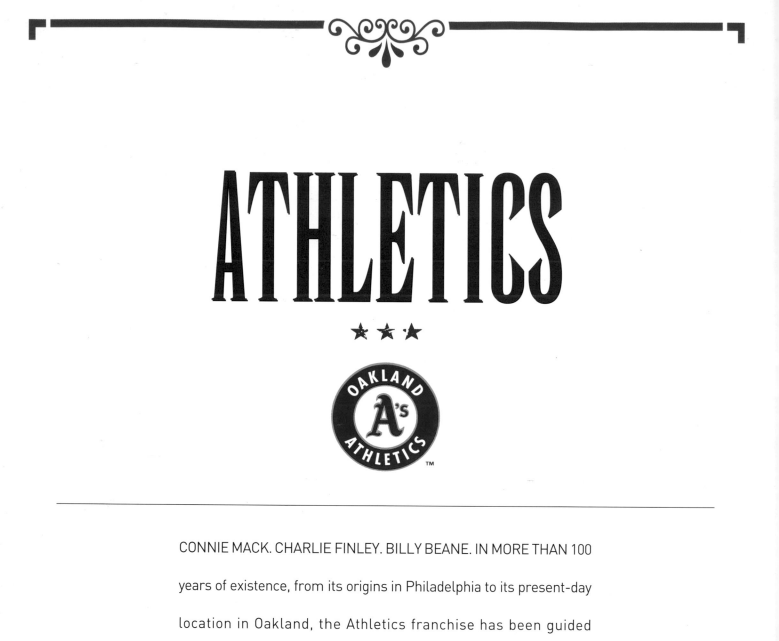

CONNIE MACK. CHARLIE FINLEY. BILLY BEANE. IN MORE THAN 100 years of existence, from its origins in Philadelphia to its present-day location in Oakland, the Athletics franchise has been guided by some of the most brilliant and controversial figures in the history of baseball. One thing that cannot be disputed, however, is the franchise's long record of success, including four World Series championships and 13 division titles in Oakland. From creative hurlers Lefty Grove and Catfish Hunter to Reggie Jackson and Rickey Henderson, the A's have always been powered by colorful stars whose box-office appeal was matched only by their box-score success.

REGGIE JACKSON

- ★ 1973 AL MVP and World Series MVP
- ★ Won four home run crowns
- ★ Hit 37 home runs by the 1969 All-Star break
- ★ Smashed 520-foot home run during 1971 All-Star Game
- ★ Stole home during 1972 ALCS

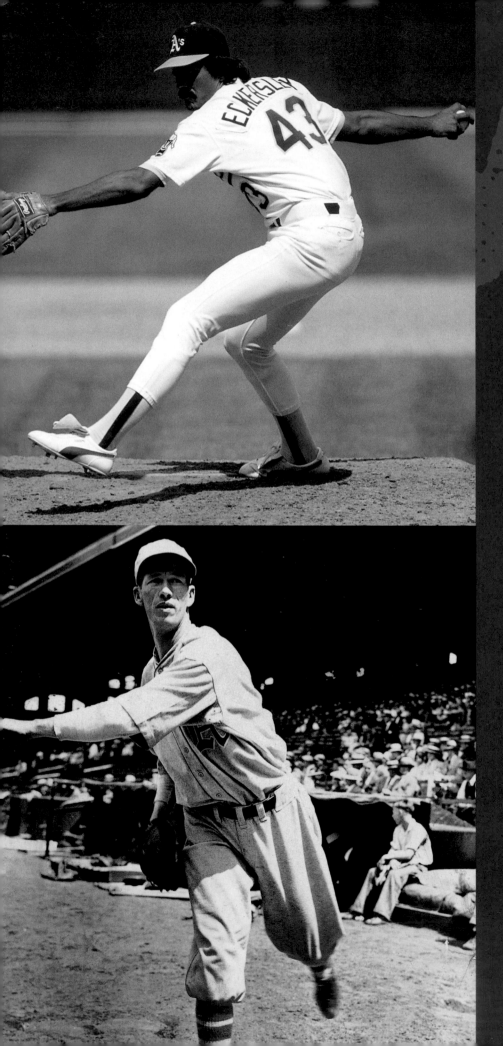

DENNIS ECKERSLEY

★ 1992 AL MVP and Cy Young Award winner

★ Owns three best single-season saves totals in club history

★ Posted 0.61 ERA in 1990

★ Saved all four games of the 1988 ALCS

★ Inducted into Baseball Hall of Fame in 2004

LEFTY GROVE

★ Won pitching's Triple Crown in 1930 and 1931

★ 1931 AL MVP

★ Won Major League–record nine ERA titles

★ Won 20 or more games seven straight seasons

★ Inducted into Baseball Hall of Fame in 1947

RICKEY HENDERSON

★ 1990 AL MVP

★ Stole 100 or more bases three times in four-year span

★ Holds Major League records for career runs and stolen bases

★ Batted .441 during 1989 post-season

★ Hit Major League–record 81 career leadoff home runs

CATFISH HUNTER

★ 1974 AL Cy Young Award winner

★ Posted combined 4-0 record in 1972, 1973 and 1974 World Series

★ Tossed perfect game on May 8, 1968

★ Won 20 or more games five straight seasons

★ Uniform No. 27 retired in 1993

BLUE JAYS

★ ★ ★

BASEBALL MAY BE AMERICA'S PASTIME, BUT CANADA'S LARGEST

city has staked its own claim to the sport during its first 30 years

in the Major Leagues. Toronto captured two world titles—becoming

the first team outside of the U.S. to win a crown in 1992—and five

division titles, while leading the AL in attendance seven times.

Befitting a modern-day cosmopolitan metropolis, Toronto's success

has been fueled by an international panoply of stars, including

Americans Joe Carter, Dave Stieb and Vernon Wells; Puerto Ricans

Jose Cruz Jr., Carlos Delgado and Roberto Alomar; and an influx of

Dominicans such as Juan Guzman, George Bell and Tony Fernandez.

JOE CARTER

* Walk-off home run in Game 6 clinched 1993 World Series title

* Holds AL record with five three-homer games

* In April 1994, set Major League record with 31 RBI

* Drove in 100 or more runs 10 times in 12-year span

* Homered twice in both 1992 and 1993 World Series

ROBERTO ALOMAR

★ 10-time Gold Glove Award winner

★ 1992 ALCS MVP

★ 12-time All-Star

★ Holds club record with lifetime .307 batting average

★ Batted .480 during 1993 World Series

TONY FERNANDEZ

★ Won four consecutive Gold Gloves

★ Batted .333 with 9 RBI in 1993 World Series

★ Five-time All-Star

★ Holds single-season club record with 17 triples

★ Led AL shortstops in putouts three times

PAT HENTGEN

★ 1996 Cy Young Award winner

★ Three-time All-Star

★ Led AL in innings pitched in 1996 and 1997

★ Tossed 40 consecutive scoreless innings in 1997

★ Became second 20-game winner in club history in 1996

DAVE STIEB

★ Tossed no-hitter on September 2, 1990

★ Once lost no-hitters in the 9th inning in consecutive starts

★ Led AL in ERA in 1985

★ Started All-Star Game in 1983 and 1984

★ Holds club record with 175 career wins

BRAVES

★ ★ ★

THE ONLY FRANCHISE TO WIN A WORLD CHAMPIONSHIP IN three different cities (Boston, Milwaukee and Atlanta), the Braves have enjoyed their most remarkable success over the past 16 seasons, winning 14 division titles, four pennants and one World Series championship. During that impressive run, Braves fans came out to see one of the best pitching rotations ever assembled, featuring Cy Young Award winners Tom Glavine, Greg Maddux and John Smoltz. But individual greatness is nothing new for this franchise, which also happens to boast one of the most dominant left-handers of all time and the all-time home run king.

HANK AARON

★ Holds Major League career marks for home runs and RBI

★ 1957 NL MVP

★ Won NL batting titles in 1956 and 1959

★ Lifetime .362 hitter in postseason

★ Inducted into Baseball Hall of Fame in 1982

CHIPPER JONES

★ 1999 NL MVP

★ Hit 13 career postseason home runs

★ Drove in 100 or more runs eight straight seasons

★ Five-time All-Star

★ Selected first overall in 1990 First-Year Player Draft

PHIL NIEKRO

★ Tossed no-hitter on August 5, 1973

★ Won 1967 NL ERA title

★ Led NL in innings pitched four times

★ Won 268 games in Braves uniform

★ Inducted into Baseball Hall of Fame in 1997

JOHN SMOLTZ

★ 1996 NL Cy Young Award winner

★ Led NL in wins in 1996

★ Led NL in saves in 2002

★ 1992 NLCS MVP

★ Lifetime 15-4 record in post-season through 2005

WARREN SPAHN

★ Holds record for most wins by left-hander in MLB history

★ 1957 Major League Cy Young Award winner

★ Won 20 or more games 13 times

★ Tossed two career no-hitters

★ Inducted into Baseball Hall of Fame in 1973

BREWERS

★ ★ ★

IT WOULD HAVE BEEN UNDERSTANDABLE IF MILWAUKEE FANS

had carried a grudge against baseball after the Braves' successful

tenure in the city ended with the team's bitter departure for Atlanta

in 1966. But when Major League Baseball returned to the Cream

City in 1970, Brewers fans showed their civic pride by supporting

the home team through thick and thin, all the while developing

a well-deserved reputation for throwing the best tailgate parties in

the Bigs. It's that unique character that has helped Milwaukee

fans foster a special bond with their players, especially with

the versatile shortstop from California known simply as "The Kid."

★ 1982 and 1989 AL MVP

★ Holds club records for home runs and RBI

★ Never played in the Minor Leagues

★ Recorded 3,000th career hit on September 9, 1992

★ Inducted into Baseball Hall of Fame in 1999

ROBIN YOUNT

CECIL COOPER

★ Batted .300 or better seven straight seasons

★ Hit three home runs in a game on July 27, 1979

★ Led AL in RBI in 1980 and 1983

★ Won two Gold Glove Awards

★ Drove in winning run in Game 5 of 1982 ALCS

ROLLIE FINGERS

★ Won 1981 AL MVP and Cy Young awards

★ Posted ERA below 2.00 in 1981 and 1984

★ Seven-time All-Star

★ Held career saves record upon his retirement in 1985

★ Uniform No. 34 retired in 1992

JIM GANTNER

★ Played entire 17-year career with Milwaukee

★ Led AL second basemen in double plays twice

★ Holds club record with 106 career sacrifices

★ Batted .333 in 1982 World Series

★ Ranks third on Brewers' all-time games-played list

PAUL MOLITOR

★ Hit safely in 39 consecutive games in 1987

★ Seven-time All-Star

★ Batted club-record .353 in 1987

★ Holds club record with 136 runs scored in 1982

★ Inducted into Baseball Hall of Fame in 2004

CARDINALS

★ ★ ★

AS THE MOST DECORATED FRANCHISE IN NL HISTORY, THE

St. Louis Cardinals have been fueled by a gallery of brilliant pitchers,

sluggers and defensive specialists, ranging from the irrepressible Dizzy

Dean to the intimidating Bob Gibson, from the powerful Joe Medwick

to the near-superhuman Albert Pujols, and from the dazzling Marty

Marion to the incomparable Ozzie Smith. In the Cards' history, they

have been blessed with a unique bond between their players and their

fans. Although Branch Rickey brought the franchise a steady supply

of talent when he invented the farm system, the club's devoted fan

base has ensured that much of its homegrown talent stays in St. Louis.

★ Three-time NL MVP

★ Won seven NL batting crowns

★ 24-time All-Star

★ Collected 3,000th career hit on May 13, 1958

★ Inducted into Baseball Hall of Fame in 1969

STAN MUSIAL

LOU BROCK

- 1967 World Series MVP
- Swiped record seven stolen bases in 1967 and 1968 World Series
- Collected 3,000th career hit on August 13, 1979
- Stole NL-record 118 bases in 1974
- Inducted into Baseball Hall of Fame in 1985

- ★ 1968 NL MVP
- ★ 1968 and 1970 NL Cy Young Award winner
- ★ Struck out a World Series–record 35 batters in 1968
- ★ Pitched no-hitter on August 14, 1971
- ★ Inducted into Baseball Hall of Fame in 1981

BOB GIBSON

ALBERT PUJOLS

★ 2005 NL MVP

★ 2001 NL Rookie of the Year

★ Won NL batting crown in 2003

★ Led NL in runs scored three straight seasons

★ 2004 NLCS MVP

- Won 13 Gold Glove Awards
- Homered off Tom Niedenfuer to win 1985 NLCS
- 15-time All-Star
- Led NL shortstops in assists eight times
- Inducted into Baseball Hall of Fame in 2002

OZZIE SMITH

CUBS

★ ★ ★

SPORTSWRITER JOE S. JACKSON ONCE OBSERVED THAT IN Chicago, "Baseball is a religion rather than a sport." If Jackson is right, then the faith of Cubs fans has been sorely tested over the years, as the franchise has now gone 98 seasons since last winning a world championship in 1908. Despite a long string of failure and frustration, the enthusiasm of Cubs fans has never waivered; in fact, the club seems to be *gaining* fans, as evidenced by the sellouts at Wrigley Field. The city's love affair with iconic figures like Harry Caray, Ron Santo and Ernie Banks complements the persistent optimism expressed in the perennial call to "wait 'til next year."

ERNIE BANKS

★ 1958 and 1959 NL MVP

★ 13-time All-Star

★ Led NL in home runs in 1958 and 1960

★ Belted 500th career home run on May 12, 1970

★ Inducted into Baseball Hall of Fame in 1977

★ 1971 NL Cy Young Award winner
★ Won 20 or more games six straight seasons
★ Holds club record with 2,038 career strikeouts
★ Homered six times during 1971 season
★ Inducted into Baseball Hall of Fame in 1991

FERGUSON
JENKINS

- ★ **1984 NL MVP**
- ★ **Nine-time Gold Glove Award winner**
- ★ **Hit NL-best 40 home runs in 1990**
- ★ **Lifetime .385 hitter in postseason**
- ★ **Inducted into Baseball Hall of Fame in 2005**

RYNE SANDBERG

RON
SANTO

★Hit 20 or more home runs nine straight seasons
★Five-time Gold Glove Award winner
★Led NL in on-base percentage in 1964 and 1966
★Led NL third basemen in assists seven times
★Uniform No. 10 retired in 2003

- ★ 1961 NL Rookie of the Year
- ★ Played in 1,117 consecutive games
- ★ Won 1972 NL batting crown with .333 mark
- ★ Hit 20 or more home runs 13 straight seasons
- ★ Inducted into Baseball Hall of Fame in 1987

BILLY WILLIAMS

DEVIL RAYS

★ ★ ★

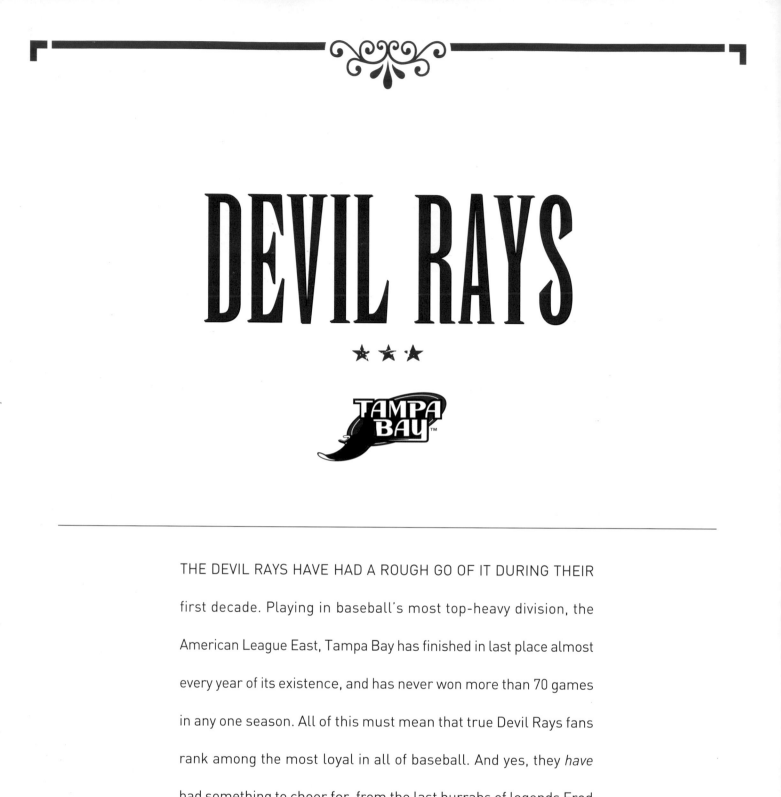

THE DEVIL RAYS HAVE HAD A ROUGH GO OF IT DURING THEIR

first decade. Playing in baseball's most top-heavy division, the

American League East, Tampa Bay has finished in last place almost

every year of its existence, and has never won more than 70 games

in any one season. All of this must mean that true Devil Rays fans

rank among the most loyal in all of baseball. And yes, they *have*

had something to cheer for, from the last hurrahs of legends Fred

McGriff and Wade Boggs to the energizing emergence of young

stars Scott Kazmir and Carl Crawford. Given the frustrations

of the past, the future in Tampa Bay looks increasingly bright.

WADE BOGGS

★ Homered on August 7, 1999, to join the 3,000-hit club

★ Hit first home run in club history on March 31, 1998

★ Batted .301 in final Big League season

★ Named All-State kicker for Tampa's Plant High School

★ Uniform No. 12 retired in 2000

CARL CRAWFORD

★ Stole club-record 59 bases in 2004

★ Named to 2004 All-Star team

★ Led AL in stolen bases in 2003 and 2004

★ Led AL in triples in 2004 and 2005

★ Offered scholarship to play basketball at UCLA

ROBERTO HERNANDEZ

★ Holds franchise record with 101 career saves

★ Saved club record 43 games in 1999

★ Earned 200th career save on May 1, 1999

★ Named to 1999 All-Star team

★ Set AL record by saving 62.3 percent of team's wins in 1999

AUBREY HUFF

★ Holds club record with 128 career home runs

★ Drove in more than 100 runs in 2003 and 2004

★ Batted better than .310 in 2002 and 2003

★ Hit safely in eight straight plate appearances in 2004

★ Stole home on September 6, 2003

FRED McGRIFF

★ Hit 400th career home run on June 2, 2000

★ Collected 2,000th career hit on June 4, 2000

★ One of only six players to homer off 300 different pitchers

★ Five-time All-Star

★ Starred for Jefferson High School in Tampa

DIAMONDBACKS

★ ★ ★

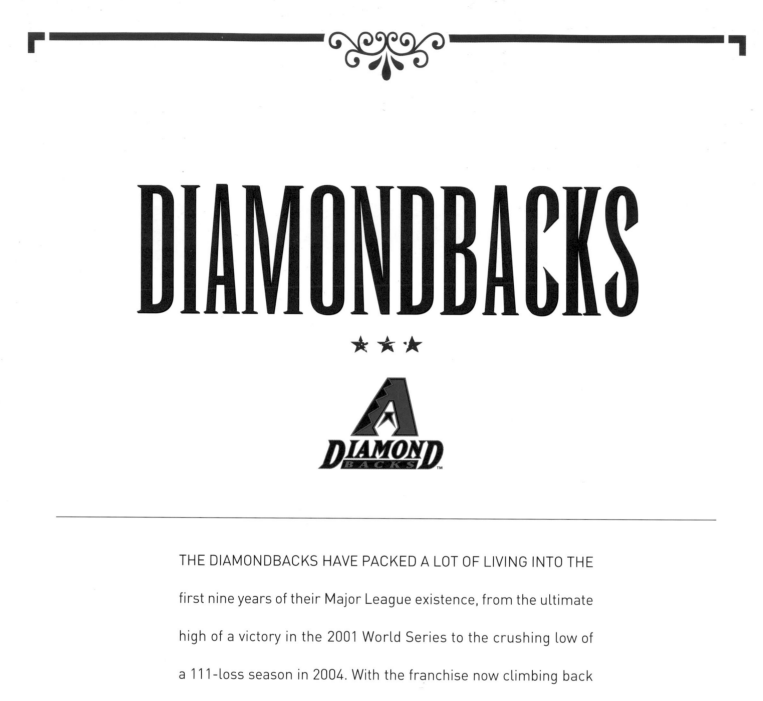

THE DIAMONDBACKS HAVE PACKED A LOT OF LIVING INTO THE first nine years of their Major League existence, from the ultimate high of a victory in the 2001 World Series to the crushing low of a 111-loss season in 2004. With the franchise now climbing back into contention, a glance back at the club's history reveals the blossoming of Luis Gonzalez, a superstar who was supposed to be past his prime; the dominant, inspired pitching of Curt Schilling during his three-plus seasons with the franchise; and the brilliant reign of left-handed fireballer Randy Johnson, whose signing in December 1998 ranks as one of the best free-agent deals in history.

★ Four-time NL Cy Young Award winner

★ 2001 World Series co-MVP with three victories

★ Led NL in strikeouts five times

★ Won three NL ERA titles

★ Tossed perfect game on May 18, 2004

RANDY JOHNSON

JAY BELL

★ Scored winning run in Game 7 of 2001 World Series

★ Holds club record with 132 runs scored in 1999

★ Named to 1999 All-Star team

★ 38 home runs in 1999, second on club to Luis Gonzalez

★ Hit a grand slam in 1999 that won a fan $1 million

LUIS GONZALEZ

★ Drove in winning run in Game 7 of 2001 World Series

★ Set club record with 57 home runs in 2001

★ Five-time All-Star

★ Holds club record for career home runs and RBI

★ Reeled off 30-game hitting streak in 1999

TODD STOTTLEMYRE

★ Won Game 2 of 1999 NLDS

★ Like older brother, Mel Jr., played collegiate ball at UNLV

★ Combined with father, Mel, to win 302 games

★ Won 2000 Branch Rickey Award for charity work

★ Lifetime .577 winning percentage with Arizona

MATT WILLIAMS

★ Set club record with 142 RBI in 1999

★ Drove in seven runs in 2001 World Series

★ Five-time All-Star

★ Batted .375 in 1999 NLDS

★ Hit 300th career home run on April 7, 1999

DODGERS

★ ★ ★

ONE OF BASEBALL'S HALLMARK FRANCHISES, THE DODGERS HAVE

earned a special place in the history of the sport as the pre-eminent

October challengers to the Yankees. First in Brooklyn, then in L.A.,

the Dodgers became the anti-Yankees, the champs for the rest of

America. That the "Boys of Summer" won just three of their 11 Fall

Classic encounters with New York only has enhanced their appeal to

a country that loves to root for the underdog. In the Dodgers' history,

they have boasted some of the most culturally significant players of

all time, including the hard-throwing left-hander from Brooklyn and

the fiery Californian who broke baseball's color barrier in 1947.

★ Broke baseball's color barrier on April 15, 1947

★ 1949 NL MVP

★ 1947 Major League Rookie of the Year

★ Stole home during Game 1 of 1955 World Series

★ Inducted into Baseball Hall of Fame in 1962

JACKIE ROBINSON

ROY CAMPANELLA

★ Three-time NL MVP

★ Led NL backstops in putouts six times

★ Drove in NL-best 142 runs in 1953

★ MVP of 1941 Negro Leagues All-Star Game

★ Inducted into Baseball Hall of Fame in 1969

★ **Three-time Cy Young Award winner**
★ **1963 NL MVP**
★ **Won pitching's Triple Crown three times**
★ **Pitched perfect game on September 9, 1965**
★ **Inducted into Baseball Hall of Fame in 1972**

SANDY KOUFAX

PEE WEE REESE

★ 10-time All-Star

★ Batted .345 in 1952 World Series

★ Led NL shortstops in putouts four times

★ Scored NL-best 132 runs in 1949

★ Inducted into Baseball Hall of Fame in 1984

★ Homered four times during 1952 World Series

★ Led NL in runs scored three straight seasons

★ Slugged NL-best 43 home runs in 1956

★ Holds club record with 389 career home runs

★ Inducted into Baseball Hall of Fame in 1980

DUKE SNIDER

GIANTS

★ ★ ★

WHEN THE GIANTS MOVED FROM NEW YORK TO SAN FRANCISCO

following the 1957 season, the city on the Bay did not merely inherit

a great baseball franchise. Rather, it continued a flourishing

baseball tradition for which San Francisco was already famous.

Prior to the Giants' arrival on the West Coast, the city had been

home to such Major League stars as Joe DiMaggio, Harry Hooper,

Tony Lazzeri, Lefty O'Doul and Joe Cronin. During the Giants'

five decades in San Francisco, they have continued to add to this

legacy with a steady stream of new generations of superstars,

from Willie Mays and Willie McCovey to Will Clark and Barry Bonds.

★ 1954 and 1965 NL MVP

★ Led NL in home runs four times

★ 12-time Gold Glove Award winner

★ Homered four times in a game on April 30, 1961

★ Inducted into Baseball Hall of Fame in 1979

WILLIE MAYS

- ★ Seven-time NL MVP
- ★ Hit Major League-record 73 home runs in 2001
- ★ Holds single-season slugging and on-base percentage records
- ★ Batted .471 with four home runs during 2002 World Series
- ★ Intentionally walked 120 times during 2004 season

BARRY BONDS

- Won 20 or more games six times
- Captured NL ERA title in 1969
- Led NL in shutouts in 1965 and 1969
- Pitched no-hitter on June 15, 1963
- Inducted into Baseball Hall of Fame in 1983

JUAN MARICHAL

WILLIE McCOVEY

- 1969 NL MVP
- Hit 500th career home run on June 30, 1978
- 1959 NL Rookie of the Year
- Led NL in home runs three times
- Inducted into Baseball Hall of Fame in 1986

MEL OTT

- Led NL in home runs six times

- Holds franchise record with 1,860 career RBI

- Batted .389 during 1933 World Series

- Led National League in on-base percentage four times

- Inducted into Baseball Hall of Fame in 1951

INDIANS

★ ★ ·★

WITH ONLY TWO WORLD CHAMPIONSHIPS IN THE FRANCHISE'S first 106 seasons, Cleveland fans have grown accustomed to the gallows humor that shadows the team and was the inspiration for the 1989 film *Major League*. But perhaps longtime Cleveland sportswriter Gordon Cobbledick said it best when he wrote of the Indians, "They may...have been a headache, but they were never a bore." Indeed, from the defensive wizardry of Tris Speaker and Kenny Lofton to the slugging exploits of Napoleon Lajoie and Jim Thome, Indians fans always have had plenty of reasons to come out to the park, and perhaps none better than the fireballing right-hander from Iowa.

BOB FELLER

★ Won pitching's Triple Crown in 1940

★ Led AL in wins six times

★ Tossed three career no-hitters

★ Holds club record for career wins and strikeouts

★ Inducted into Baseball Hall of Fame in 1962

EARL AVERILL

★ Holds franchise record with 1,084 career RBI

★ Batted .378 in 1936

★ Lifetime .322 hitter in Indians uniform

★ Batted better than .300 six straight seasons

★ Inducted into Baseball Hall of Fame in 1975

LARRY DOBY

★ First African American to play in American League

★ Led AL in home runs in 1952 and 1954

★ Seven-time All-Star

★ Drove in more than 100 runs five times

★ Inducted into Baseball Hall of Fame in 1998

NAPOLEON LAJOIE

- ★ Won Triple Crown in 1901
- ★ Batted .426 in 1901, highest in AL history
- ★ Won five AL batting crowns
- ★ Led AL second basemen in double plays six times
- ★ Inducted into Baseball Hall of Fame in 1939

TRIS SPEAKER

- ★ 1912 AL MVP
- ★ Holds Major League record with 792 doubles
- ★ Managed Indians to 1920 world championship
- ★ Led AL outfielders in putouts seven times
- ★ Inducted into Baseball Hall of Fame in 1939

MARINERS

★ ★ ★

OVER THE LAST 12 SEASONS, THE MARINERS HAVE ERASED AN

early history marked by frustration and mediocrity. Fueled by a

new generation of stars, they have become a force in the AL

West, posting an AL-record 116-win season in 2001 and winning

three division titles. Despite the new heights to which Japanese

sensation Ichiro Suzuki has taken them, the club's greatest moment

undoubtedly remains its thrilling comeback in the 1995 AL Division

Series, capped by Edgar Martinez's game-winning double in the

11th inning of Game 5, which plated Ken Griffey Jr. and sent the

city of Seattle into a frenzy from which it still has yet to fully recover.

★ 1997 AL MVP

★ Led AL in home runs four times

★ Won 10 consecutive Gold Glove Awards

★ Set club record with 147 RBI in 1997

★ 1992 All-Star Game MVP

KEN GRIFFEY JR.

JAY BUHNER

★ Hit 40 or more home runs in three straight seasons

★ Won Gold Glove Award in 1996

★ Batted .458 during 1995 ALDS

★ Hit for cycle on June 23, 1993

★ Traded to Mariners for Ken Phelps in 1988

EDGAR MARTINEZ

★ Holds club record with 1,261 RBI

★ Won AL batting crowns in 1992 and 1995

★ Seven-time All-Star

★ Led AL in RBI in 2000

★ Batted .571 during 1995 ALDS

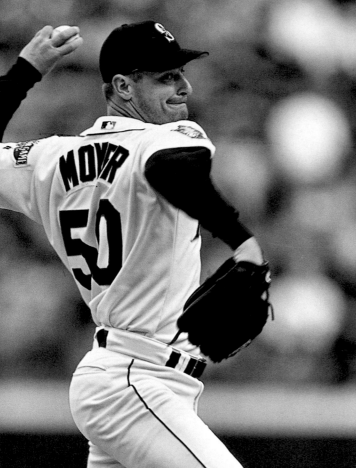

JAMIE MOYER

★ At 38, became oldest first-time 20-game winner in 2001

★ Won 200th career game on July 8, 2005

★ Named to first All-Star team at age 40

★ Went 2-0 in 2001 ALDS

★ Led AL in winning percentage in 1996

ICHIRO SUZUKI

★ 2001 AL MVP and Rookie of the Year

★ Won 2001 and 2004 AL batting crowns

★ Five-time Gold Glove Award winner

★ Set Major League record with 262 hits in 2004

★ Batted .600 in 2001 ALDS

MARLINS

★ ★ ★

IT WAS UNDOUBTEDLY AN OPTIMIST WHO SAID, "ON OPENING

day, everybody is in first place." A cheerful sentiment, and one

amply supported by the chaotic history of the Marlins, who have

twice shocked the baseball world with improbable runs to the title.

Even more impressive, the Marlins' two championship teams arrived

just six years apart but featured entirely different casts: The 1997

squad was led by veterans Kevin Brown and Gary Sheffield, while

the 2003 team was anchored by youngsters Josh Beckett and Miguel

Cabrera. Perhaps the strongest link between the two champs was

Jeff Conine, the unassuming utility player known as "Mr. Marlin."

DONTRELLE WILLIS

★ **2003 NL Rookie of the Year**

★ **Became Marlins' first 20-game winner in 2005**

★ **Two-time All-Star**

★ **Led NL in shutouts and complete games in 2005**

★ **Batted .261 during 2005 season**

WILLIS

35

JOSH BECKETT

★ 2003 World Series MVP

★ Pitched shutout to win Game 6 of 2003 World Series

★ Selected second overall in 1999 amateur draft

★ Struck out 12 batters on July 21, 2002

★ 1999 *USA Today* High School Pitcher of the Year

LUIS CASTILLO

★ Led NL in stolen bases in 2000 and 2002

★ Holds club record with 35-game hitting streak in 2002

★ Three-time Gold Glove Award winner

★ Three-time NL All-Star

★ Holds franchise record with 1,273 career hits

JEFF CONINE

★ 1995 All-Star Game MVP

★ Batted .458 during 2003 NLCS

★ Two-time NL All-Star

★ Selected by Marlins in 1992 expansion draft

★ Batted career-best .319 in 1994

ROBB NEN

★ Holds club record with 108 career saves

★ Posted 1.95 ERA in 1996

★ Saved 35 games in both 1996 and 1997

★ Collected four saves during 1997 postseason

★ Son of former Major Leaguer Dick Nen

METS

★ ★ ★

DURING THE 1960s, THE NEW YORK METS WENT FROM BEING

the worst team in baseball to the absolute best. But perhaps what

was most "Amazin'" about these Mets was not their players but

their fans, who found room in their hearts for both Tom Terrific

and Marvelous Marv Throneberry. During the years that followed,

Mets fans have continued to embrace both their superstars and

the role players who give the team its character. It would be wrong to

think that Mets history is just about the Mike Piazzas and Dwight

Goodens, when it's also about the Mookie Wilsons and John Fran-

cos—blue-collar players who reflect the city's working-class roots.

TOM SEAVER

★ Three-time Cy Young Award winner
★ Holds club record with 198 career wins
★ Won three NL ERA titles
★ 1967 NL Rookie of the Year
★ Inducted into Baseball Hall of Fame in 1992

JOHN FRANCO

★ Led NL in saves three times

★ Holds club record for career saves

★ Four-time All-Star

★ Ranks second all-time in games pitched

★ Recorded 400th career save on April 14, 1999

TUG McGRAW

★ Coined 1973 rallying cry "Ya Gotta Believe"

★ Winning pitcher in 1972 All-Star Game

★ Lifetime 2.24 ERA in postseason

★ Saved nine games in September 1973

★ Led NL in winning percentage in 1971

MIKE PIAZZA

★ Most home runs by catcher in Major League history

★ 12-time All-Star

★ Led club in home runs four times

★ Batted .412 during 2000 NLCS

★ Set club record with 124 RBI in 1999

DARRYL STRAWBERRY

★ Holds club record with 252 career home runs

★ 1983 NL Rookie of the Year

★ Led NL in home runs in 1988

★ Eight-time All-Star

★ First overall pick in 1980 First-Year Player Draft

NATIONALS

★ ★ ·★

DON'T BE FOOLED BY THE NEW UNIFORMS. IN ITS HISTORY, THE nation's capital has been home to some of baseball's most significant figures. Hall of Famer Clark Griffith managed, then owned, the city's AL entry. Walter Johnson brought the city its first title in 1924, and even Ted Williams spent time at the helm. D.C. also has a connection to the Senior Circuit: Washington had an NL entry from 1891 to 1999. That team never finished with a winning record, but with one .500 season already under their belt, the Nationals—who made D.C. their home in 2005, after 36 years in Montreal—now stand poised to add another memorable chapter to the city's baseball legacy.

GARY CARTER

★ 1981 and 1984 All-Star Game MVP

★ Led NL in RBI in 1984

★ Three-time Gold Glove Award winner

★ Batted .438 during 1981 NLCS

★ Inducted into Baseball Hall of Fame in 2003

LIVAN HERNANDEZ

★ Led NL in innings pitched three straight seasons

★ Two-time All-Star

★ Opening Day starter for Nationals in 2005

★ Batted .244 with two home runs in 2005

★ Led 2005 Nationals in wins

BRIAN SCHNEIDER

★ Threw out 38 percent of base stealers in 2005

★ Set club record with .998 fielding percentage in 2004

★ Hit two home runs on April 18, 2003

★ Hit career-best 12 home runs in 2004

★ Player of the Year in Lehigh Valley (PA) 1994–95

RUSTY STAUB

★ Six-time All-Star

★ First Expo to hit 30 home runs in a season

★ Nicknamed "Le Grande Orange"

★ Holds club record with career .402 OBP

★ Uniform No. 10 retired by Expos in 1993

JOSE VIDRO

★ Three-time All-Star

★ Batted career-best .330 in 2000

★ Scored more than 100 runs in 2000 and 2002

★ Hit career-best 51 doubles in 2000

★ Won Silver Slugger Award in 2003

ORIOLES

★ ★ ★

PERHAPS NO TOWN IN THE MAJOR LEAGUES UNDERSTANDS

what it means to be a Hometown Hero better than the Charm City.

The birthplace of Babe Ruth and Al Kaline, Baltimore's love affair

with its baseball team has fostered some of the most unique

player-fan relationships in the history of the game. During the

1960s and '70s, untold numbers of Maryland kids were named

Brooks, after the team's brilliant third baseman. A succeeding

generation developed its own special bond with the star shortstop

who played every day and who, on September 6, 1995, repaid the

fans for their kindness with an unforgettable jog around the park.

CAL RIPKEN JR.

★ Played in 2,632 consecutive games

★ 1983 and 1991 AL MVP

★ 1982 AL Rookie of the Year

★ Holds career record for home runs by a shortstop

★ Collected 3,000th career hit on April 15, 2000

EDDIE MURRAY

★ Third player to join 500 home runs, 3,000 hit club

★ 1977 AL Rookie of the Year

★ Hit 500th career home run on September 6, 1996

★ Homered twice in Game 5 of 1983 World Series

★ Inducted into Baseball Hall of Fame in 2003

JIM PALMER

★ Won three AL Cy Young Awards

★ Holds club record with 268 career wins

★ Eight-time 20-game winner

★ Hurled no-hitter on August 13, 1969

★ Inducted into Baseball Hall of Fame in 1990

BROOKS ROBINSON

★ 16-time Gold Glove Award winner
★ 1964 AL MVP
★ 1970 World Series MVP
★ 18-time All-Star
★ Inducted into Baseball Hall of Fame in 1983

FRANK ROBINSON

★ Won Triple Crown in 1966
★ 1966 AL MVP
★ 1966 World Series MVP
★ 1989 AL Manager of the Year
★ Inducted into Baseball Hall of Fame in 1982

PADRES

★ ★ ·★

PLAYING IN ONE OF THE MOST BEAUTIFUL CITIES IN THE UNITED

States, San Diego's baseball team has been an integral part of

the city's landscape since the days when a young Ted Williams

starred for the Padres of the Pacific Coast League. Since joining

the National League, the organization has been home to a host

of memorable personalities, including broadcaster Jerry Coleman,

who cheered fine plays by waving a gold star from the press box.

But no Padre has been as beloved as the peerless Tony Gwynn,

a native Californian who spent 20 seasons with the club, helping

the team to its first two National League pennants in 1984 and 1998.

★ Eight-time NL batting champion

★ Batted .394 in 1994

★ Five-time Gold Glove Award winner

★ Collected 3,000th career hit on August 6, 1999

★ Uniform No. 19 retired in 2002

TONY GWYNN

BRIAN GILES

★ Led NL in walks in 2005

★ Led Padres with .423 OBP in 2005

★ 2005 Padres team MVP

★ Reached base safely in 13 straight plate appearances in 2005

★ Drove in seven runs on May 17, 2006

TREVOR HOFFMAN

★ Four-time All-Star

★ Led NL in saves in 1998

★ Was on pace to claim all-time saves record in 2006

★ Saved 41 consecutive games from 1997 to 1998

★ Recorded 400th career save on May 6, 2005

RANDY JONES

★ 1976 NL Cy Young Award winner

★ First Padre to reach 20 wins in a season

★ Holds club record with 18 career shutouts

★ Led NL in ERA in 1975

★ Uniform No. 35 retired in 1997

DAVE WINFIELD

★ Twelve-time All-Star

★ Seven-time Gold Glove Award winner

★ Led NL in RBI in 1979

★ Never played in the Minor Leagues

★ Inducted into Baseball Hall of Fame in 2001

PHILLIES

★ ★ ★

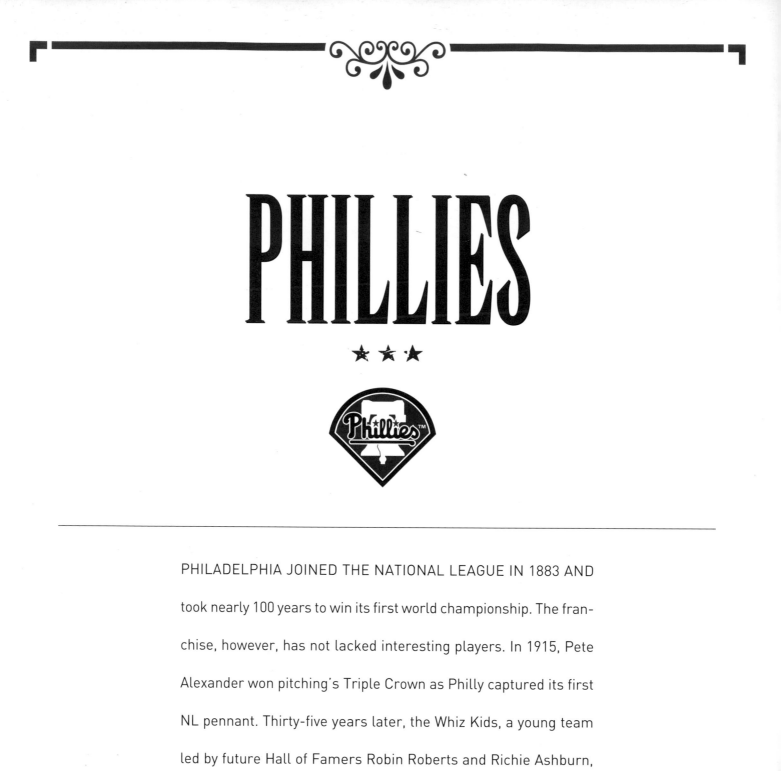

PHILADELPHIA JOINED THE NATIONAL LEAGUE IN 1883 AND

took nearly 100 years to win its first world championship. The fran-

chise, however, has not lacked interesting players. In 1915, Pete

Alexander won pitching's Triple Crown as Philly captured its first

NL pennant. Thirty-five years later, the Whiz Kids, a young team

led by future Hall of Famers Robin Roberts and Richie Ashburn,

drove the Phillies to a narrow pennant victory over Brooklyn. But

the franchise's greatest triumph came in 1980, when a veteran

team, led by its slick-fielding, power-hitting third baseman, finally

brought a World Series title home to the City of Brotherly Love.

★ Three-time NL MVP

★ 1980 World Series MVP

★ 10-time Gold Glove Award winner

★ Led NL in home runs eight times

★ Inducted into Baseball Hall of Fame in 1995

MIKE SCHMIDT

RICHIE ASHBURN

★ Won two NL batting crowns

★ Led NL in walks four times

★ Led NL outfielders in putouts nine times

★ Five-time All-Star

★ Inducted into Baseball Hall of Fame in 1995

STEVE CARLTON

★ Four-time NL Cy Young Award winner

★ Won pitching's Triple Crown in 1972

★ Led NL in strikeouts five times

★ Holds franchise record with 241 career wins

★ Inducted into Baseball Hall of Fame in 1994

CHUCK KLEIN

★ Won 1933 NL Triple Crown

★ 1932 NL MVP

★ Led NL in home runs four times

★ Hit four homers in a game on July 10, 1936

★ Inducted into Baseball Hall of Fame in 1980

ROBIN ROBERTS

★ Led NL in wins four straight seasons

★ Led NL in innings pitched five straight seasons

★ Holds club record with 272 career complete games

★ Led NL in strikeouts in 1953 and 1954

★ Inducted into Baseball Hall of Fame in 1976

PIRATES

★ ★ ★

DESPITE AN IMPRESSIVE RESUME, PITTSBURGH OFTEN HAS BEEN

the NL's Rodney Dangerfield, with its many on-field accomplishments

overlooked by a national sports media more attuned to the east and

west coasts. Honus Wagner was arguably the most valuable player in

baseball history, but his name is conspicuously absent from most de-

bates on the subject. While for Roberto Clemente, it took a brilliant

performance during the 1971 World Series to land him on the national

radar. Although the rest of the baseball world may have been slow to

notice, Pittsburgh fans have shown their gratitude, cheering their team

through five World Series championships and nine NL pennants.

★ 1966 NL MVP

★ 12-time Gold Glove Award winner

★ 1971 World Series MVP

★ Recorded 3,000th career hit on September 30, 1972

★ Inducted into Baseball Hall of Fame in 1973

ROBERTO CLEMENTE

RALPH KINER

★ Won seven straight NL home run titles

★ Six-time All-Star

★ Hit three homers in a game four times

★ Led NL in runs scored in 1951

★ Inducted into Baseball Hall of Fame in 1975

BILL MAZEROSKI

★ Hit walk-off home run to win 1960 World Series

★ Eight-time Gold Glove Award winner

★ Led NL second basemen in double plays eight times

★ Nine-time All-Star

★ Inducted into Baseball Hall of Fame in 2001

WILLIE STARGELL

★ 1979 NL co-MVP

★ Holds club records for career home runs and RBI

★ 1979 NLCS and World Series MVP

★ Led NL in home runs twice

★ Inducted into Baseball Hall of Fame in 1988

HONUS WAGNER

★ Eight-time NL batting champion

★ Led NL in slugging percentage six times

★ Led NL in stolen bases five times

★ Holds NL record for career triples

★ Inducted into Baseball Hall of Fame in 1939

RANGERS

★ ★ ★

ARLINGTON, TEXAS, HAS BEEN A HAVEN FOR HOME RUN HITTERS,

thanks to the region's heat and the somewhat favorable dimensions

of Arlington Stadium and, later, the Ballpark at Arlington (known

today as Ameriquest Field). During the last three decades, Rangers

fans have seen memorable bashers like Jeff Burroughs, Ruben

Sierra, Juan Gonzalez and Mark Teixeira. Despite the fans'

appetite for the longball, though, the undisputed fan favorite player

has been hard-throwing Texas native Nolan Ryan, who joined the

club at age 42 and proceeded to shock the baseball world by

tossing his record-shattering sixth and seventh career no-hitters.

- Led AL in strikeouts in 1989 and 1990
- Pitched sixth career no-hitter on June 11, 1990
- Pitched seventh career no-hitter on May 1, 1991
- Won 300th career game on July 30, 1990
- Inducted into Baseball Hall of Fame in 1999

NOLAN RYAN

RUSTY GREER

★ Scored more than 100 runs three straight seasons

★ Drove in 100 or more runs three times

★ Batted .332 in 1996

★ Hit career-best 26 home runs in 1997

★ Lifetime .305 batting average

IVAN RODRIGUEZ

★ 1999 AL MVP

★ Holds club record with 1,723 career hits

★ 11-time Gold Glove Award winner

★ Batted .300 or better eight straight seasons

★ Recorded career-best 85 assists in 1992

JIM SUNDBERG

★ Six-time Gold Glove Award winner

★ Three-time All-Star

★ Recorded career-best 103 assists in 1977

★ Led AL backstops in assists six times

★ Second on Rangers' all-time games played list

MARK TEIXEIRA

★ Holds record for most RBI by a switch-hitter

★ Led AL in total bases in 2005

★ Won 2005 Gold Glove Award

★ Hit for the cycle on August 17, 2004

★ Hit three homers in a game on July 13, 2006

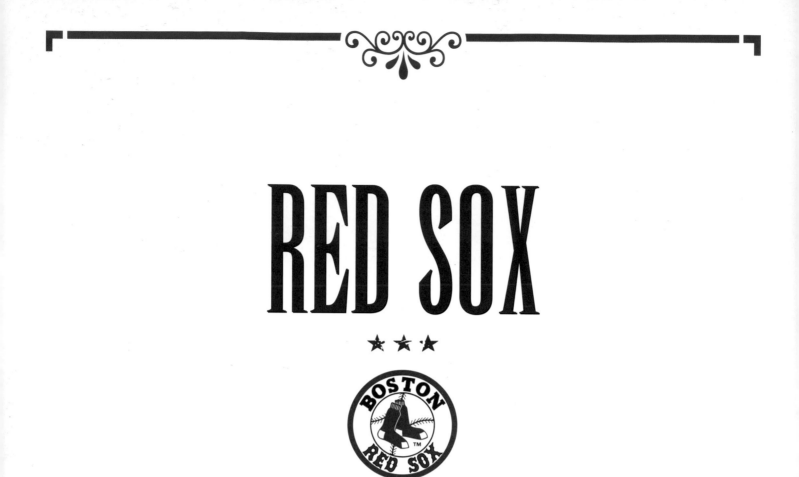

RED SOX

★ ★ ·★

BEFORE THE INFAMOUS "CURSE," THE RED SOX WERE THE BEST

franchise in baseball, winning five titles between 1903 and 1918.

Then came a series of unforgettable heartbreaks: 1946, 1967, 1978,

1986 and 2003, until they finally ended the drought in 2004. To get that

close to triumph that often and come up short, you need great

players, and the Red Sox have had them—from the lanky power-

hitter from San Diego to the strapping son of a Long Island potato

farmer. "Baseball isn't a life-and-death matter," sportswriter Mike

Barnicle once observed, "but the Red Sox are." Nobody knows the

truth of that statement better than Beantown's Hometown Heroes.

TED WILLIAMS

★ Won 1942 AL Triple Crown
★ 1946 and 1949 AL MVP
★ Six-time AL batting champion
★ Batted .406 in 1941
★ Inducted into Baseball Hall of Fame in 1966

★ **1986 AL MVP**

★ **Won three Cy Young Awards with club**

★ **Holds club record with 2,590 career strikeouts**

★ **Led AL in shutouts six times**

★ **Struck out 20 batters in a game in 1986 and 1996**

ROGER CLEMENS

JIM RICE

★ **1978 AL MVP**

★ **Led AL in home runs three times**

★ **Eight-time All-Star**

★ **Posted four 200-hit seasons**

★ **Won International League Triple Crown in 1974**

CARL YASTRZEMSKI

★ Won 1967 AL Triple Crown

★ 1967 AL MVP

★ Three-time AL batting champion

★ Seven-time Gold Glove Award winner

★ Inducted into Baseball Hall of Fame in 1989

- ★ Holds Major League record with 511 wins
- ★ Won pitching's Triple Crown in 1901
- ★ Pitched perfect game on May 5, 1904
- ★ Led AL in wins three straight seasons
- ★ Inducted into Baseball Hall of Fame in 1939

CY YOUNG

REDS

THE QUEEN CITY'S PROFESSIONAL BASEBALL HISTORY STRETCHES

back further than any other, to the powerhouse 1869 team led by

brothers George and Harry Wright, which set the stage for the

emergence of the NL seven years later. Since joining the Senior

Circuit for good in 1890, the Reds have featured an assortment of

colorful characters—from pitchers Dolf Luque and Rob Dibble to

sluggers Ernie Lombardi and Ted Kluszewski. But none have been

more memorable than the sparkplugs that fired the Big Red Machine

during the 1970s, including catcher Johnny Bench, first baseman Tony

Perez, second baseman Joe Morgan and jack-of-all-trades Pete Rose.

★1973 NL MVP

★Holds Major League record with 4,256 career hits

★1963 NL Rookie of the Year

★Hit safely in 44 consecutive games in 1978

★1975 World Series MVP

PETE ROSE

★1970 and 1972 NL MVP
★10-time Gold Glove Award winner
★1976 World Series MVP
★1968 NL Rookie of the Year
★Inducted into Baseball Hall of Fame in 1989

JOHNNY BENCH

JOE MORGAN

★ 1975 and 1976 NL MVP

★ Won five consecutive Gold Gloves

★ Holds club record with .415 career OBP

★ Drove in winning run in Game 7 of 1975 World Series

★ Inducted into Baseball Hall of Fame in 1990

TONY PEREZ

★ Seven-time All-Star
★ Drove in more than 100 runs eight times
★ Hit 40 home runs in 1970
★ Homered to win 1967 All-Star Game
★ Inducted into Baseball Hall of Fame in 2000

★ 1961 NL MVP

★ Led NL in slugging percentage three straight seasons

★ 1956 NL Rookie of the Year

★ Hit three homers in a game August 22, 1959

★ Uniform No. 20 retired in 1998

FRANK ROBINSON

ROCKIES

★ ★ ★

ALTHOUGH ORGANIZATIONAL SUCCESS HAS LARGELY ELUDED

the Rockies since they joined the National League in 1993, a

number of hitters have revived their careers playing in the thin

air of the Mile High City. The best bashers, however, have been

those who earned their stripes playing in more conventional envi-

ronments, such as Andres Galarraga and Larry Walker, who helped

Colorado to its first playoff appearance in the 1995 National League

Division Series. In more recent years, the franchise has been led

by Todd Helton, the athletic first baseman who entered the 2006

season with the highest career batting average of any active player.

- ★ 1997 NL MVP
- ★ Seven-time Gold Glove Award winner
- ★ Three-time NL batting champion
- ★ Holds record for most career home runs by a Canadian-born player
- ★ Five-time All-Star

LARRY WALKER

DANTE BICHETTE

★ Led NL in home runs and RBI in 1995

★ Four-time All-Star

★ Holds club record with 219 hits in 1998

★ Hit for cycle on June 10, 1998

★ Batted .588 in 1995 NLDS

VINNY CASTILLA

★ Hit 40 or more home runs three straight seasons

★ Smashed three homers in a game on June 5, 1999

★ Holds record for most career home runs by a Mexican-born player

★ Batted better than .300 five straight seasons

★ Two-time All-Star

ANDRES GALARRAGA

★ Led NL in home runs and RBI in 1996

★ Holds club record with 150 RBI in 1996

★ Hit three homers in a game on June 25, 1995

★ Five-time All-Star

★ Smashed a 529-foot home run on May 31, 1997

TODD HELTON

★ Won 2000 NL batting crown

★ Led NL in on-base percentage in 2000 and 2005

★ Three-time Gold Glove Award winner

★ Holds club records for career home runs and RBI

★ Hit for cycle on June 19, 1999

ROYALS

★ ★ ★

KANSAS CITY HAS A NOBLE BASEBALL TRADITION DATING BACK

to the glory days of the Kansas City Monarchs of the Negro Leagues,

who dominated with great pitching from Satchel Paige and Bullet

Joe Rogan, and excellent speed and defense from Newt Allen and

Cool Papa Bell. The Royals followed a similar formula to great

success during the 1970s and 1980s, when the franchise won seven

division titles and a world championship with help from the pitching

of Bret Saberhagen and Dan Quisenberry, the speed and defense

of Willie Wilson and Frank White, and the beautiful swing of the

greatest Kansas City player of them all—third baseman George Brett.

★ 1980 AL MVP

★ Won AL batting crowns in 1976, 1980 and 1990

★ Lifetime .337 hitter in the postseason

★ Collected 3,000th career hit on September 30, 1992

★ Inducted into Baseball Hall of Fame in 1999

GEORGE BRETT

AMOS OTIS

★ Led AL in doubles in 1970 and 1976

★ Five-time All-Star

★ Batted .478 during 1980 World Series

★ Three-time Gold Glove Award winner

★ Led AL in stolen bases in 1971

BRET SABERHAGEN

★ 1985 and 1989 AL Cy Young Award winner

★ 1985 World Series MVP

★ Holds club record with 23 wins in 1989

★ Pitched no-hitter on August 26, 1991

★ Three-time All-Star

MIKE SWEENEY

★ Five-time All-Star
★ Holds club record with 144 RBI in 2000
★ Three-time Royals Player of the Year
★ Hit safely in 25 consecutive games in 1999
★ Batted career-best .340 in 2002

FRANK WHITE

★ Eight-time Gold Glove Award winner
★ 1980 ALCS MVP
★ Hit for cycle in 1979 and 1982
★ Led AL second basemen in fielding percentage three times
★ Uniform No. 20 retired in 1995

TIGERS

★ ★ ★

DETROIT WAS CONSIDERED THE AMERICAN LEAGUE'S WEAKEST

link in 1901, but by the end of the decade, both the city and its

baseball franchise had experienced a renaissance: Henry Ford

started producing his Model T cars in 1908, just as a young Georgian

was making Detroit the center of the baseball universe. Fiery,

aggressive and brilliant on the bases and at the plate, Ty Cobb was

baseball's biggest attraction, leading the Tigers to three pennants

from 1907 to 1909. Detroit has not seen anything like Cobb since,

but thanks to stars like Hank Greenberg, Al Kaline and Alan

Trammell, it has remained one of the league's signature franchises.

TY COBB

★ Holds Major League record with .366 career average

★ Won 1909 Triple Crown

★ 1911 AL MVP

★ 11-time AL batting champion

★ Inducted into Baseball Hall of Fame in 1939

CHARLIE GEHRINGER

- ★ 1937 AL MVP
- ★ Led AL second basemen in assists seven times
- ★ Lifetime .320 batting average
- ★ Batted .375 during 1935 World Series
- ★ Inducted into Baseball Hall of Fame in 1949

HANK GREENBERG

- ★ 1935 and 1940 AL MVP
- ★ Led AL in home runs four times
- ★ Drove in club-record 183 runs in 1937
- ★ Homered to clinch 1945 AL pennant
- ★ Inducted into Baseball Hall of Fame in 1956

AL KALINE

★ Won 1955 AL batting crown at age 20

★ 10-time Gold Glove Award winner

★ Holds club record with 399 career home runs

★ Collected 3,000th career hit on September 24, 1974

★ Inducted into Baseball Hall of Fame in 1980

ALAN TRAMMELL

★ 1984 World Series MVP

★ Four-time Gold Glove Award winner

★ Batted career-best .343 in 1987

★ Six-time All-Star

★ Three-time Silver Slugger Award winner

TWINS

★ ★ ★

THE TWINS WASTED LITTLE TIME PUTTING THEIR IMPRINT

on the former Washington Senators, leading the AL in attendance

twice in their first five seasons in Minnesota and culminating with

the pennant-winning 1965 campaign. That team, led by the hitting

of Harmon Killebrew and Tony Oliva, set the tone for the decades

that followed. The Twins won seven division titles, aided in no small

part by the Metrodome, which became the loudest stadium in

baseball when packed with Homer Hanky–waving Twins fans. Tak-

ing full advantage of the unique environment, the legendary Kirby

Puckett inspired the club to two improbable titles in 1987 and 1991.

KIRBY
PUCKETT

- ★ Led AL in hits four times
- ★ Six-time Gold Glove Award winner
- ★ Homered to win Game 6 of 1991 World Series
- ★ 1989 AL batting champion
- ★ Inducted into Baseball Hall of Fame in 2001

ROD CAREW

★ 1977 AL MVP
★ Seven-time AL batting champion
★ 1967 AL Rookie of the Year
★ Holds franchise record with career .334 average
★ Inducted into Baseball Hall of Fame in 1991

KENT HRBEK

★ Second-most career home runs in franchise history
★ Hit 20 or more home runs 10 times
★ Selected to AL All-Star team in 1982
★ Graduate of Kennedy High School in Bloomington, Minn.
★ Uniform No. 14 retired in 1995

HARMON KILLEBREW

★ 1969 AL MVP

★ Led AL in home runs six times

★ Holds franchise records for career home runs and RBI

★ Hit 500th career home run on August 10, 1971

★ Inducted into Baseball Hall of Fame in 1984

TONY OLIVA

★ Three-time AL batting champion

★ 1964 AL Rookie of the Year

★ Holds club record with 374 total bases in 1964

★ Led AL in doubles four times

★ Uniform No. 6 retired in 1991

WHITE SOX

★ ★ ★

EXPLODING SCOREBOARDS, DISCO DEMOLITION NIGHTS AND playing baseball wearing shorts. For a storied franchise that won the American League's first pennant as a major league in 1901, the White Sox have built a reputation for gimmickry and innovation, and have attracted some of the game's most unique personalities, from Bill Veeck to Minnie Minoso and Ozzie Guillen. Yet the franchise's most beloved players also include the silent-but-steady types, most notably longtime catcher Carlton Fisk and Harold Baines, the beloved designated hitter who spent three tours of duty with the club during his 22 years in the Bigs—and showed that you *can* come home again.

FRANK THOMAS

★ 1993 and 1994 AL MVP

★ Led AL in on-base percentage four times

★ Holds club record with 448 career HR

★ Won 1997 AL batting crown

★ Drove in more than 100 runs eight straight seasons

LUKE APPLING

★ Two-time AL batting champion

★ Holds club record with 2,749 career hits

★ Seven-time All-Star

★ Led AL shortstops in assists seven times

★ Inducted into Baseball Hall of Fame in 1964

HAROLD BAINES

★ Six-time All-Star

★ Drove in more than 100 runs three times

★ Batted .300 or better eight times

★ Hit three homers in a game in 1982 and 1984

★ Uniform No. 3 retired in 1989

NELLIE FOX

★ 1959 AL MVP

★ Led AL in hits four times

★ Led AL second basemen in putouts 10 straight seasons

★ 14-time All-Star

★ Inducted into Baseball Hall of Fame in 1997

MINNIE MINOSO

★ Led AL in stolen bases three times

★ Three-time Gold Glove Award winner

★ 10-time AL hit-by-pitch leader

★ Played in five different decades

★ Uniform No. 9 retired in 1983

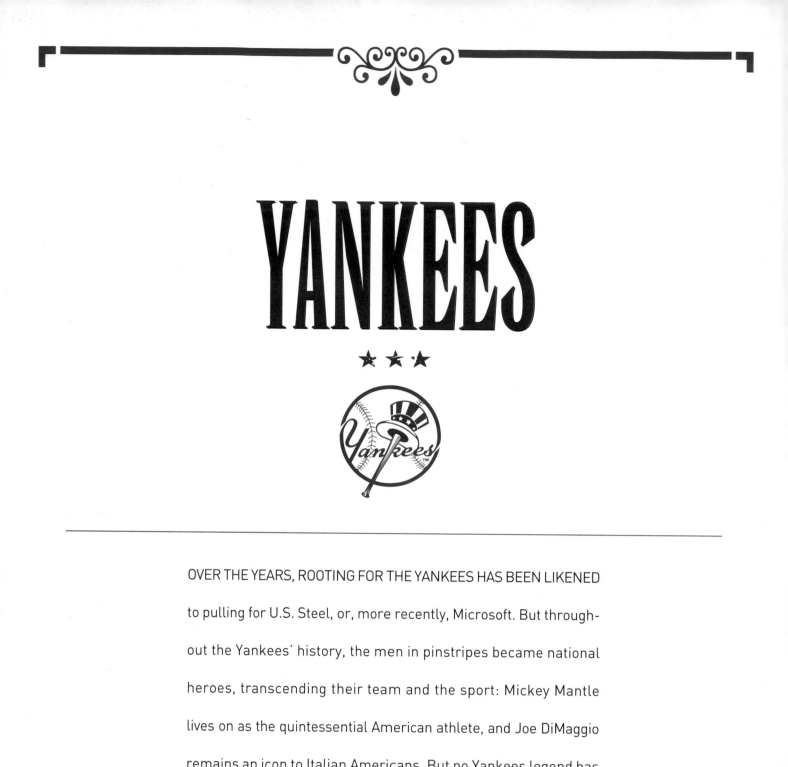

YANKEES

★ ★ ★

OVER THE YEARS, ROOTING FOR THE YANKEES HAS BEEN LIKENED

to pulling for U.S. Steel, or, more recently, Microsoft. But through-

out the Yankees' history, the men in pinstripes became national

heroes, transcending their team and the sport: Mickey Mantle

lives on as the quintessential American athlete, and Joe DiMaggio

remains an icon to Italian Americans. But no Yankees legend has

the cultural currency of Babe Ruth, whose larger-than-life

personality and mammoth home runs came to define the Jazz

Age and remain a potent symbol of the American Century.

★ Led AL in home runs 12 times

★ Hit 15 home runs in World Series

★ Led AL in slugging percentage 13 times

★ Broke own record with 60 home runs in 1927

★ Inducted into Baseball Hall of Fame in 1939

BABE RUTH

YOGI BERRA

★ Three-time AL MVP

★ Hit three home runs in the 1956 World Series

★ Hit 20 or more home runs 10 straight seasons

★ Won 10 world titles with the Yankees

★ Inducted into Baseball Hall of Fame in 1972

JOE DiMAGGIO

★ Major League–record 56-game hitting streak in 1941

★ Three-time AL MVP

★ Won AL batting titles in 1939 and 1940

★ Led AL in home runs and RBI twice each

★ Inducted into Baseball Hall of Fame in 1955

★ Won Triple Crown in 1934

★ 1927 and 1936 AL MVP

★ Batted .545 with four home runs in 1928 World Series

★ Played in 2,130 consecutive games

★ Inducted into Baseball Hall of Fame in 1939

LOU GEHRIG

MICKEY MANTLE

★ Won Triple Crown in 1956

★ Three-time AL MVP

★ Led AL in runs scored six times

★ Hit 500th career home run on May 14, 1967

★ Inducted into Baseball Hall of Fame in 1974

CURTAIN CALL

★ ★ ★

★ ★ ★